Billy Flint's
Hobby Hill

Billy Flint's
Hobby Hill

by
Seena Karen Rasmussen Drapala

With memories shared from:

Bob Schierbaum & Louisa Alger Watrous

First Printing: 2021

ISBN 978-1-6671-2750-7

Library of Congress Control Number 2021915593

Ordering Information:

U.S. trade bookstores and wholesalers: Please contact:
Seena Karen Rasmussen Drapala
Tel: 775 781 5491;
email seena.drapala@gmail.com.

Dedication

For Billy,
a family friend, beloved "Tante", mentor,
and inspiration on how to live a full life,
no matter what comes your way.

Lillian J. Flint

Jan 5, 1904 - Dec 23, 1994

Contents

Acknowledgments

Much of the history about Billy was compiled by Connie Craver, dated January 1984, and presented to me after Billy's death by Beulah H. Hagadorn, another family friend and long-time roommate of Billy's.

I would like to thank my mother, Helene Rasmussen, for capturing the photographs and creating a scrapbook of almost 100 photos from Hobby Hill Camp. My grandmothers; Karen Valborg Sofie Rasmussen & Sine Sorensen Christensen Hansen, were also friends of Billy and strong female role models, captured here in photographs.

To Louisa Watrous, who connected with me on Ancestry.com while looking for Lillian Flint, and to Bob Schierbaum, a childhood neighbor and friend, and long-lost fellow ballroom dance classmates, thank you, for sharing your stories about Billy and her ballroom dance classes.

Book cover credit goes to Lisa Frisch whose artistic talents are amazing and never cease to deliver. Thanks also to John Green for some photographic clean up.

During my research I was helped by many librarians and historians. Thanks to Elizabeth McCollum, Historical Society of Windham County Museum in Newfane Vermont, for access to Lewis R. Brown's photos of Hobby Hill; to Marietta Carr, Schenectady County Historical Society, for Larry Hart's "Tales of Old Dorp" article in their Flint Family files; and to Beverly Clark, Village of Scotia, for opening the Flint House.

I did not do this research alone. My able "assistant", Deborah Drapala, was always at my side, up for any adventure! Thanks so much, Deb.

A special thanks goes to Erica Walch, the current proprietor of Hobby Hill and director of the Moore Free Library & Crowell Art Gallery in Newfane, Vermont… without whose prodding and help, this book would not have been completed. Thank you for your patience and inspiration.

Preface

This book is the result of finding my mother's scrapbook which included photographs of her wedding to my father on 2nd of September, 1939 and numerous photos of the Hobby Hill Camp in Newfane, Vermont. Only a few of the people in the photographs are known to me. Having known Billy Flint (Lillian J. Flint) as a Danish Sisterhood Society "sister", family friend, and beloved "Tante" I did not have the heart to throw out such treasures. My hope is that others will find friends and relatives among these photo treasures.

Billy was at ease with young and old. She was a marketing master, conveyer of social graces, mentor, friend, confidante, poet, photographer, artist, musician, lover of old houses; antiques, stamp, and coin collector, as well as, a player in the stock market, just to name a few of her interests.

Billy traveled to Denmark with my grandmother Val in 1956. In the 1970's Billy invited me to join Schenectady Photographic Society when I graduated from high school and was working at General Electric. Our lives were so entwined and I was so inspired by her person.

The photographs at Hobby Hill represent a period in our U.S. World War II history from a uniquely female perspective, I had to write this book.

I have attempted to portray an overview of what Hobby Hill camp life included by sharing the various photographs of camp activities. I have also captured what I know of Billy's life from the early years, her ballroom instructor activities with personal accounts, Hobby Hill, her entrepreneur endeavors with "Gifts from the Heart", stories and photos from her photographic period, as well as, her later life and her legacy of the Flint House, to provide a fuller view of this amazing woman.

Introduction Poems

Poems by Karen Valborg Sofia Rasmussen

We take a trip to Hobby Hill - To Billy

There is something so grand in the Vermont air
When skies are blue and the weather fair,
Winding roads and rippling brooks
Like something out of story books.

Beautiful scenery wherever you gaze
Pastures so green, where the cattle graze,
A horse silhouetted against the sky,
Standing at ease on a hill so high.

A woody trail up to Hobby Hill Camp
Where we stretch our legs as the woods we tramp
thru a shady lane where the breeze is cool
we find our way to the swimming pool.

Girlish voices and laughter so gay
Ring out so clear on a summer day
Happy groups just everywhere
of lucky girls, who can play up here.

No wonder you love Vermont my dear
Contentment is in the atmosphere.

First to Bennington, then over the Molly Stark Trail
to Billy Flint's farm "Hobby Hill", Newfane Vermont.
Elsie, Norma, Emma, Anne & Valborg.
Aug 7 – 8, 1937

"A Trip to Vermont"

We started early one summer-day
On a trip to where ever we please
The party was happy, with laughter gay
While we drove along at our ease.

A winding trail among mountain and hill,
Where each turning brings beauty untold,
The heart at such wonder gets many a thrill,
Watching each new view unfold.

Stately old trees so majestically stand,
Reaching high into clear skies of blue,
Reflected in lakes make a picture so grand,
We were awed with the beauty anew.

A village with houses so friendly and gay
The lawns were like carpets so fine;
Gardens with flowers and children at play,
Tall background of maple and pine.

A church in the valley next meets our gaze,
The bells ringing out soft and mellow,
Pastures where cattle so peacefully graze,
Stone fences and cornfields so yellow.

2

Chapter 1: Early Years

Erie, Pennsylvania 1904 to 1937

Billy Flint was born Lillian Joan Flint on January 5th, 1904, the oldest child of George and Marie Flint of Erie, Pennsylvania. She was followed by two brothers, Amos on October 18, 1906, and Howard H. Flint on August 15, 1910. Billy's mother was of Danish descent. This made her "family" when she relocated to Schenectady, New York where my family lived. The Danish Sisterhood and Danish Brotherhood Societies connected fellow Danes together.

She preferred to be called Billy. She was 'Tante Billy' to me, pronounced "ten-ta", which means aunt in Danish. She was not a real aunt but such a close family friend that my dad teased her and called her 'Sis'. Thus, Billy became my Tante Billy for all her years.

Billy spent her early years in Erie. She was a violinist in the Erie Philharmonic and a string quartet. She went to Dennison University in Granville, Ohio to study music, later switching to physical education, studying gymnastics at Arnold College in New Haven, Connecticut. After earning a Bachelor of Science in Physical Education from the University of Pittsburgh she studied gymnastics under Niels Bukh at People's College, Ollerup, Denmark and Germany.

She returned to Erie to teach junior high school and later became the YWCA Health Education Director there. She also led Athletics and Aquatics for Erie County Sunday School Summer Camp in North Gerard, PA and Pennsylvania State Sunday School Association.

In 1931 Billy moved to Schenectady to become the newly opened YWCA Health Education Director, a position she held for seven years. She also spent four summers at Camp Englenook at Mariaville, New York. She lived at the YWCA for a while before moving to 14 Mohawk Ave, Scotia, NY where she lived above the Scotia Library.

All these experiences set her up to start Hobby Hill Camp in Newfane, Vermont on July 1st, 1935. A girls' summer camp that she would operate for twenty years. See Chapter 3. Area parents asked Billy to incorporate dance classes into the YW education program. When the dance master, Van Arnem from Troy, was too busy to teach, Billy took some time off to get trained and tried her hand at teaching dance. (credit: Larry Hart – Tales of Old Dorp, September 18, 1984). Thus, starting her new career in dance.

Chapter 2: Ballroom Dancing

Schenectady, New York from 1938 to 1964

Newly minted Dancing Master of America and a member of Dance Educators of America headquartered in New York, New York, Billy took the very popular dance classes out on her own.

Billy became legendary in Schenectady, New York for her ballroom dance classes and cotillions she started in 1938. She started teaching at the Hotel Van Curler, later moved to Shaughnessy Hall and the old Friendly Social Club in Scotia. She taught all ages from tinies to debutantes for at least 25 seasons. This was her winter activity and Hobby Hill Camp was her summer endeavor.

Billy never had children of her own but I imagine all the dance students were certainly looked upon fondly. My brother and I were lucky enough to be of the age to attend these dress-up ballroom dance lessons. Traveling from Guilderland in the country to downtown Schenectady for lessons, I felt so grown up! Billy was always dressed in the most beautiful gowns. I am sure she arranged for me in the picture to be published in the Schenectady Gazette highlighting her dance classes. How special I felt being included in the newspaper!

A childhood friend and neighbor of mine, Bob Schierbaum, recalls "I know that I went to dance lessons with Billy in Schenectady. My lasting memory of dance was when we had a dance off. The dancers were eliminated so that the best dancer won. I remember the girl I danced with but I have no idea what her name was. They kept eliminating dancers and we kept dancing. It came down to two couples and the other couple was eliminated. We won! As a reward we each got a silver dollar. I may still have it today. As a side note I wore a cross pin on my sport coat that day. Thereafter I always wore it to dance. I never won again. I know that I danced with that same girl again but it wasn't the same. I always wore a sport coat and I held a handkerchief on her back I guess that was the custom. I have no idea how old we were when we went there. I think the dance hall was on second floor but I could be mistaken."

Louisa Alger Watrous remembered "Billy had a social dance class in Schenectady for young people, that Mom attended, and I did, too, when I was in about 5th grade. We got dressed up and wore white gloves."

I personally remember lining up with boys on one side and girls on the other side. That is how we paired up for dancing. Billy was always so much fun. She was so outgoing, friendly, and creative.

Another of Billy's creative arts was poetry:

Dawn

Punctual, tidy, housewife, Dawn,

Unfailingly each day

Gets out her gaily colored rags

And dusts the Stars away.

Lillian J. Flint

The Woman's Press, a Y.W.C.A. publication, awarded her a prize in competition, as also did a publication in Erie.

Schenectady Zontians are honored to salute Billy Flint, outstanding Zontian, outstanding Schenectadian.

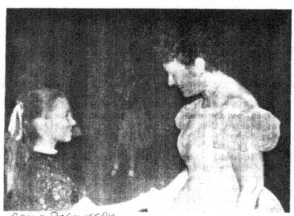

Seena Rasmussen
One of Billy's happiest moments

Chapter 3: Hobby Hill, Newfane, Vt.

Girls camp from 1935 to 1955

Billy

Informational letter to potential campers.

"Every Girl a Leader"

Lillian Joan Flint, Director

14 Mohawk Avenue
Scotia, 2, N. Y.

GREETINGS FROM HOBBY HILL:

Thank you very much for your inquiry about Hobby Hill. I am sending you our little booklet which will tell you about us.

Hobby Hill is an unusual little camp for girls between the ages of 12 and 17. It is located in the lovely Green Mountains of Vermont, four miles from the historical little village of Newfane, and 16 miles from Brattleboro. The old New England farmhouse which is the center of activities, was built about 1790. Handhewn beams are exposed, there are two large fireplaces, and the house is furnished attractively. The campers sleep in little cabins, each supervised by a counselor and junior counselor.

Our program is not regimented. It is built around the needs and interests of the teen age girl. Campers help with program planning and often take leadership responsibility. The program is balanced, and well supervised.

No two days at Hobby Hill are exactly alike. We have swimming, riding, badminton, deck tennis, hiking, archery, horseshoes, and other sports; a splendid arts and crafts program; pioneer camping; dramatics; music; creative writing; dancing; and all kinds of hobbies.

We go to auctions when they are in the vicinity; attend square dances at Mr. Charles K. Field's " Playbox " in Newfane; (he is the famous " Cheerio " of radio;) entertain interesting guests; have surprise events; participate in community activities. We also have our own garden which the campers take care of; do some canning; last summer we raised two little pigs. The campers also help with the care of the horses. No activities are compulsory or required. Campers make their own choices.

Our camp is small. We take only 50 campers for we feel that it is important to work individually with every girl.

Please do not hesitate to ask me for any further information, and references.

Hobby Hill is a camp which is sincerely interested in the personality development of each girl; the development of social relationships and the joy and adventure of living together in lovely surroundings.

Cordially yours,

Billy purchased the Newfane, Vermont property in 1934. In 1935 she established Hobby Hill girls' Camp.

Louisa Alger Watrous shared her family memories of the camp "Mom attended Hobby Hill summer camp on scholarship, as Grandma [Stella Harben] was a single Mom [Judy Harben Alger], and couldn't afford the fee. She had wonderful memories and always talked about the celebration of Christmas in July, something she wanted to do with us. Walt and I were driving through Newfane several years ago, and I wondered about the camp. We stopped for gas in town, and talked to two ladies selling raffle tickets. One said her sister was running the camp! I don't recall her name. I found the website and was delighted to learn it was still operating. I gave her my contact info. in case any photos could be found. Mom was born in 1930, so it likely was when she was still fairly young when she attended camp."

On December 16th, 1941 Billy received a Western Union telegram from her fiancé's mother "This message received from James today quote mail service will be irregular for some time Kuming is the safest place in Asia don't worry notify Billy = Mrs. Sam Wilson". Major James Wilson was listed on World War II Tablets of the Missing Manila American Cemetery & Memorial Manila, Republic of the Philippines. Billy had a Newsweek article from 1942 stating the Lt. Col. James Wilson of the United States Army was directing the railroad construction from Rangoon to Chungking in Burma. Billy's fiancé was a West Point graduate.

Billy closed the camp in 1955 and sold the Hobby Hill property in 1960 to Red Chaffee and Marion Drake. They ran the place as Hobby Hill Lodge for some number of years, but not as a camp.

The following are a collection of photographs from, my mother, Helene Rasmussen's photo album. Many of the people are not known to me. I have included names when I am sure of their identity. The collection is just too wonderful not to share. I hope you find someone you know!

Billy with Grandma Val (Karen Valborg Sofie Rasmussen)

Billy Flint at Hobby Hill

Billy and Anne Brown - 1947

Billy and 'Gov' Fredrick Olaf Emil Rasmussen

The Cook?, Billy, Florence Schoenherr (my brother's godmother), & Helene Rasmussen

Dated 1947

Grandma Sine (Sorensen, Christensen, Hansen)

Left to right: Unknown, Billy, Anne Brown

Karen Valborg Sofia Rasmussen – Oregon Mountain

The clearing was a popular photographic spot.

"moin" or "mojn" meaning greeting "hello or goodbye" in Danish

Helene Rasmussen - Oregon Mountain

Elsie, Val, unknown, Norma Schlupp (Seena's godmother)

Dated 1940

norma

Lewis R. Brown photo – courtesy of Historical Society of
Windham County Museum

Eight-seater outhouse

Florence Schoenherr

Construction of the stone house

Stone house

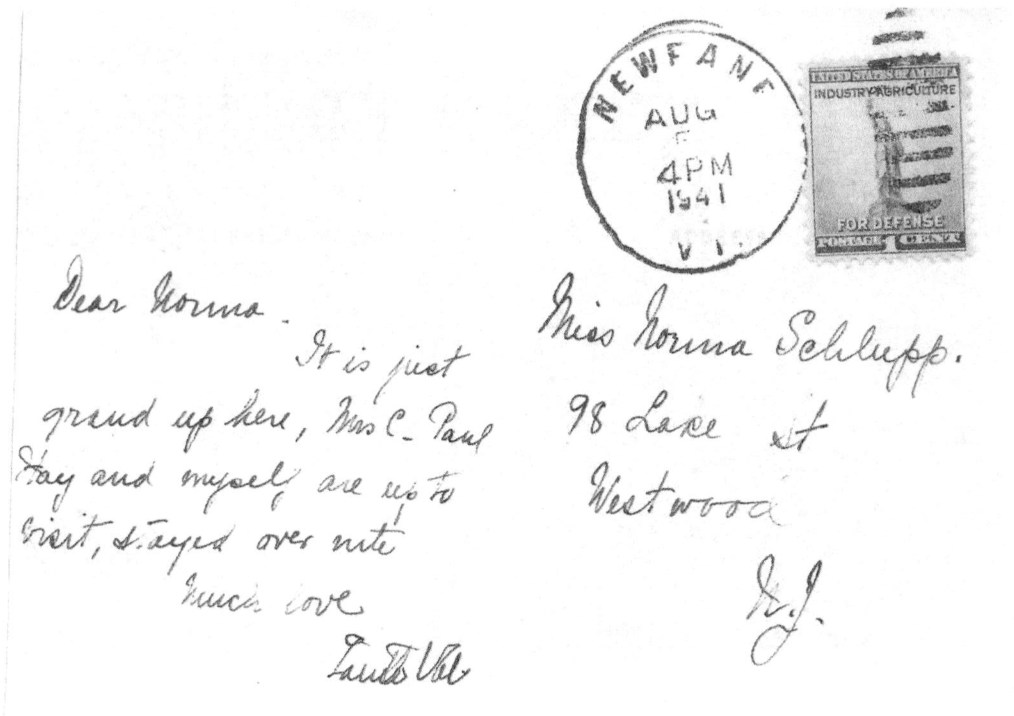

Dear Norma - It is just

grand up here, Mrs. C. Paul

Fay and myself are up to

visit, stayed over nite !

much love

Paul & Vi

Miss Norma Schlupp.

98 Lane St

Westwood

N.J.

Newfane, Vermont postcards

1941 Postcard: Billy far right top row, Helene 4th top row

Postcard to my father, Erik Rasmussen off to WWII,
from Helene, Tante Sine, and Paul (my mother,
Grandmother Sine, and Uncle Paul)

Lewis R. Brown photo – courtesy of Historical Society of
Windham County Museum

Helene Rasmussen and Margie (Hansen?)

Lewis R. Brown photo – courtesy of Historical Society of
Windham County Museum

Lewis R. Brown photo – courtesy of Historical Society of
Windham County Museum

Lewis R. Brown photo – courtesy of Historical Society of
Windham County Museum

Stone house fireplace

47

48

Lewis R. Brown image made into a postcard – courtesy
of Historical Society of Windham County Museum

Hobby Hill Camp patches

Lewis R. Brown photo – courtesy of Historical Society of
Windham County Museum

Lewis R. Brown's photographs were numbered and
several were made into postcards. He was a professional
photographer with an office at 34-36 Main Street,
Brattleboro, Vermont. The Brattleboro Historical Society
has much of his work. I hope to visit there someday.

Undoubtably, Brown's photos were used for Hobby
Hill promotional material as many photos can be found in
the brochures about the camp. Trips to Newfane,
Gloucester, and Brattleboro for art, auctions, or antiquing
are documented. Art classes, auctions, badminton, baseball,
crafts, dancing, pioneer camping, nature study, hiking,
riding, swimming, archery, fellowship, flagging, creative
writing, dramatics, music, orchestra, photography,
tournaments, trips to interesting places in New England,
surprise events, and of course sing-a-longs were all part of
camp life that the girls got to choose from.

Patches were recently found in one of the out buildings,
depicting many of these activities and archery advancement
pins from the Camp Archery Association on 152 East 22nd
Street, in New York City.

Billy was accomplished in all of these areas of interest and
would be part of her life even after Hobby Hill days.

Straight from a camp director's mouth is this tribute to the power of advertising from Miss Lillian J. Flint, director of Camp Hobby Hill, Newfane, Vt.

And Miss Flint knows whereof she speaks. For her advertising in the Camp Directory in The New York Times Magazine during the 1943 season brought her 7 enrollments—at $185 each. All this from 48 lines of advertising.

writes an advertiser in the Camp Directory
in THE NEW YORK TIMES MAGAZINE

Hobby Hill Camp advertised in
The New York Times Magazine

Hobby Hill became the Hobby Hill Lodge in the 1960's when Marion and Carleton (Red) Chafee purchased the property, hosting outdoor lovers and hunters alike for many years. Red lived there until his death in 2016 at an age of almost 101 years old.

<u>Chapter 4: Gifts from the Heart</u>

Scandinavian Imports from 1957 ~ 1966

In 1956 Billy traveled to Denmark with my Grandmother Val. I imagine that she used this trip to collect Danish treasures for her shop. They traveled by ship out of New York City and Billy returned by air. Billy's mail order business, out of her small shop in Scotia, NY, boosted 10,000 customers in 50 states!

I remember ornate white paper trees of folded paper that opened up into a beautiful Christmas tree decoration that could grace any tabletop display.

Danish plates from the Royal Copenhagen Porcelain Factory and Bing & Grondahl were among the many items for sale in her shop. The tradition started when landowners gifted their workers with food at Christmas time. Soon there was competition over who received the nicest plate. Collectibles were all the rage and these annual plates were sought. I bought my 1962 Royal Copenhagen 'The Little Mermaid in Winter' plate from Billy.

Louisa Watrous shared "Billy's mother was from Denmark, and it was her Danish roots that apparently inspired her to operate a mail order business of Danish products. …In any case, when we were kids, we got the most wonderful gifts from her at Christmas, of paper cuttings, and small elves."

Christmas would not be complete without at least one Danish Julenisse! These legendary pixie-like creatures are known for good luck and frequent mischievousness if not treated well. It is common to find them in the most unusual places each morning during the season. It is said that they are friends with the family cat.

Letters of thanks for the Julenisse that Billy sent to Walt Disney and the White House reply by Mamie D. Eisenhower follow:

WALT DISNEY

April 15, 1959

Dear Miss Flint:

Thank you for your complimentary letter of April 8th, and also, for the clever little Julenisse which you sent to me.

I hope that one day you will have the opportunity to visit Disneyland. We are quite excited about the new attractions which will be ready for our summertime visitors. However, if you should not have the chance of an actual visit, on June 15th we are televising the dedications of these attractions and you will be able to see it all on the TV screen.

Again my thanks for your thoughtfulness and my best wishes.

Sincerely,

Walt Disney

Miss Lillian J. Flint
421 Reynolds Street
Scotia 2, New York

WD:tb

WALT DISNEY
500 SOUTH BUENA VISTA ST.
BURBANK, CALIFORNIA

THE WHITE HOUSE
WASHINGTON

December 23, 1960

Dear Miss Flint,

The Danish "Julenisse" arrived to bring pleasure to the entire Eisenhower family. Thank you so much for introducing us to these delightful elves -- they have enchanted us all this Christmas Season, and you may be sure that they will continue to bring us joy in the years to come.

The President joins me in sending you our very best wishes for a happy and healthy 1961.

Sincerely,

Mamie Doud Eisenhower

Miss Lillian J. Flint
421 Reynolds Street
Scotia 2, New York

From top to bottom, left to right

Top Row

Large White paper angels. 5 inches high. 8 in package 69c
Small White paper angels. 2½ inches high. 12 in package 59c
White paper stars. 3 inches across. 8 in package 39c
White paper stars. Heavier paper. 1½ inches across V notched
for easy hanging or stringing. 12 white and 6 gold 1.00
Beautifully hand-made paper angels. Gold halos. About 3 inches
high. Really lovely. 5 in package 1.25
Mobile. Very beautiful white paper mobile with manger, sheep,
stars, birds. Hanging from crescent moons. Impressive 2.50
White paper girl with lantern. Exceptionally charming as a
tree decoration. 3 inches across. 5 in package 59c
White paper Dove of Peace. 2½ inches long. 10 in package 39c

Second Row

White paper Star-Angels. about 8 inches high. 2 in package 75c
White paper Mangers. 10½ inches high. 2 in package 1.25
Swedish Straw Angel. Hand-made and lovely. About 9 in. high 1.50
Santa Family. Delightful. Danish. handmade. All six 10.95

Elf pin. Long legs, long red cap, wooden shoes. Darling 1.25
Copper Foil Angels almost 4 inches high. American handmade
and really most charming .... pair 3.50
Copper Foil Christmas Tree loaded with tiny ornaments. American
handmade. Will give a life-time of pleasure. Exquisite.
White or green 15.00

Third Row

White paper Christmas tree. 11½ inches high with elves and geese
at bottom. Our best seller. Two in envelope $1.25; 4 trees 2.25;
6 trees 3.00; 12 trees 5.00. Sent to one address in one envelope.
Tiny Swedish Tomptes. 2½ inches tall. Chenille arms and legs.
paper head and hat. Six in package 59c
Pine cone dolls. Just adorable. Danish Handmade. Red .... Pair 1.50
Swedish Cut-out Nativity Scene about 7 inches high and 34 inches
long. Beautiful colors. A real treasure. Each 1.10
White paper tree with Angels at base. Two in package 1.25; 4 trees
2.25; 6 — 3.00; 12 trees 5.00. Sent in one package to one address
Napkin elves. Adorable. Made of rope, and wearing big wooden
shoes. Each 1.25
Swedish Straw and Wood Candle holder. 4 inches high. Very gay. Each 75c

GIFTS FROM THE HEART
P. O. Box 1197A   Scotia, N. Y.   12302

Chapter 5: Photography

Louisa Alger Watrous remembers Billy, "She also had a photography business and did portraits of us as kids. She took photos of the elves in poses with candles, with shining light, and other like arrangements. It's also divine timing being reminded of this, as a young grandson has been talking about the light, and I will share this with him, and perhaps find some of her old photos. The historical society may have some in the collection. I used to see her from time to time when I was a student at Russell Sage, from 1971-1975."

When I (the author) graduated from high school in 1970 and was working at General Electric in Schenectady, New York, Billy invited me to join the Schenectady Photographic Society where she was a member. We spent many an hour together discussing apertures f-stops, shutter speeds, lighting, composition, and debated the merits of color or black-and-white photography. My favorite memory is when she won the nude competition. A woman's bare and graceful curved back was obvious in her black-and-white photograph. Billy laughed at winning the competition and went on to explain the curious looks she received in the produce section of her local grocery store as she examined every green pepper on the shelves. The produce manager even asked if he could help her. Locating the perfect curves took time. Then staging the tabletop lighting, that she was famous for, rendered the winning photo.

She photographed glass bottles in her old house on 421 South Reynolds Street, Scotia, NY, purchased in 1952. Never a rainy day to deter her endeavors. Some of the best lighting was diffused on those cloudy days. The Danish Nisse were accomplices for many clever table top photos. Titles included: "Banana boat", "Candlelighter", and "Rainy day" shown here. I can remember another, "Crybabies" which had Nissen slicing an onion with a saw made out of a twig and string that Billy had fashioned, their tears puddling on the wooden cutting board.

There is a wonderful collection of Billy's photography at the Flint House in Scotia, New York, where you can see "Crybabies" and gifts from her shop.

"Candlelighter"

"Banana Boat"

Billy photographed visitors. My brother and I visited and received beautiful portraits taken in Billy's yard. She captured a young neighbor child holding out a bouquet of autumn flowers that she titled "Love you, Grammie".

"Love you, Grammie"

Chapter 6: Later Years

1985 ~ 1994

Billy was struck by a car when crossing the street in Scotia coming or going to the grocery store, bank, or post office. Soon after she moved to Kingsway Arms, a new assisted living facility in Schenectady, in 1985. Her infectious hearty laugh, twinkling eyes, and broad effervescent smile continued until the end.

Billy deeded her 421 S. Reynolds Street home and four acres to the Village of Scotia, New York. The history of the broomcorn farm is part mystery, murder, intrigue, and much research has been undertaken by the society. The Flint House has been opened for tours and many festivals have been held on the grounds. In 2020 it was closed due to COVID-19. The Village Historian, Beverly Clark, was gracious in providing a tour of the house when I recently visited. I hope it will again be opened on a more regular basis to share the history of the place that includes the amazing woman that led a rich life there for so many years and inspired so many by her generosity, resiliency, and talents.

Lillian Joan Flint died on December 23, 1994. She is buried with her parents in Erie, Pennsylvania at the Erie Cemetery in the Flint family plot.

1981 Billy at 421 S. Reynolds St Scotia, NY

Scotia's history in the making

Old Flint house on way to become village museum

By DANA LYNNE SINGFIELD
Gazette Reporter

SCOTIA — The stories the old Flint house could tell.

From its days as a stop for escaped slaves on the Underground Railroad to the unsolved murder that occurred in a barn on the property nearly a century ago, the 200-year-old house at the end of Reynolds Street has history seeping from its horsehair and plaster walls.

Come summer, the house may be used to tell Scotia's history if village officials successfully turn it into a museum.

The home's last owner, Lillian "Billie" Flint, left the house to the village in her will, with the request that it be used for historical purposes. Best known as a ballroom dance instructor and photographer, Flint died shortly before Christmas 1994 at the age of 90.

Village officials have since assumed custody of the house and are renovating it in phases.

The first phase will be to turn one room into a showcase for Scotia artifacts and another room into an office for village historian Michelle Norris.

"Right now [the goal] is to just get it organized and fix up the visible rooms," said village Trustee Charles F. Moehle Jr., chairman of the Flint House Committee.

Norris and her husband, Dave, are working one day a week to help restore the two-story house to its Victorian era splendor.

That is her ultimate goal: To recreate a Victorian home — right down to the wallpaper — for people to visit.

To help, the village is looking for donations of period furniture. Reptiles will do, but any gift must be in good shape, Moehle said.

Norris hopes to open the house's "museum room" in the summer.

As for remodeling the rest of the house, she and Moehle said they were unsure when that would be completed. Nor do they know if the up and coming museum will charge admission.

Moehle has a personal connection to the home.

Scotia officials want to turn the historic Flint House, above, into a museum and a reconstruction of a Victorian era home. Below, Michelle Norris, the village historian, and her husband, Dave, show off the 200-year-old house, which they are helping restore with Scotia Trustee Charles F. Moehle Jr., behind the door.

Amos K. Wise Gazette Photograph

When his father was nine years old at the turn of the century, his family lived there for three years until they built their own home.

In fact, Moehle said, one day his father had to run from the house to the village fire station — which was located then in the same place it is now on Mohawk Avenue — to try to save the burning barn behind the home.

Moehle also recalls that his father was afraid of that barn because it was there that a man was murdered a couple of years before.

Before the Moehle family moved in, the village trash man, Dave Reynolds, lived there, Norris said.

One day, Reynolds was found bludgeoned to death in the barn. His shoes were missing, and it was rumored that he hid his money there.

Reynolds' death, Norris said, remains the village's only unsolved murder.

Gazette article, undated

Epilogue:

Newfane, Vermont 2021 – beyond

Hobby Hill today is a small diversified farm offering farm products and farm stays. Erica Walch purchased the property in 2017 and has set to restoring this treasure to its utilitarian beauty. Erica is the librarian for Moore Free Library in Newfane and is capturing "Community Memory" oral history for the area. The website link is below and has interviews by Phyllis Lustig, Bev Kingsley, and myself about Hobby Hill.

I first visited Erica at the farm in July of 2019 and was graciously allowed to wander around. The drive up the hill from Newfane town square was just as I imagined a Vermont forest location would be like from my grandmother's poems that open this book. She captured the feel perfectly.

The stone house constructed by Billy is now offered for two person stays. The eight-seater outhouse was somewhat intact, there are bunkhouses, wonderful rock walls, and of course the main house where Erica lives. The fields have grown up and trees have taken over most of the view of Oregon Mountain from the road. The feel of the place is magical. Chickens, pigs, and the dogs were all such fun to see and really livened up the farm. I wish I had been old enough to attend Billy's Hobby Hill Girls Camp!

The Lewis R. Brown photographs, postcard, and a couple camp brochures reside at the Historical Society of Windham County Museum, on Route 30, in Newfane, Vermont. The museum curator, Elizabeth McCullom, was a great resource. Be sure to visit!

https://www.hobbyhill.farm
http://communitymemory.moorefreelibrary.org/

Appendix 1: Genealogy

ancestry

Lillian J Flint

BIRTH 05 JAN 1904 • Erie, Erie, Pennsylvania, USA
DEATH 23 DEC 1994 • New York, USA

Facts

Age 0 — **Birth**
05 JAN 1904 • Erie, Erie, Pennsylvania, USA

Age 2 — **Birth of Brother Amos Flint** (1906–1985)
18 October 1906 • Erie, Erie, Pennsylvania, USA

Age 6 — **Birth of Brother Howard H. Flint** (1910–1994)
15 Aug 1910 • Pennsylvania

Age 6 — **Residence**
1910 • Erie Ward 6, Erie, Pennsylvania, USA
Marital Status: Single; Relation to Head of House: Daughter

Age 16 — **Residence**
1920 • Erie Ward 5, Erie, Pennsylvania, USA
Relation to Head: Daughter; Residence Marital Status: Single

Age 19 — **Residence**
1923 • Erie, Pennsylvania, USA

Age 22 — **Death of Father George Flint** (1865–1926)
23 October 1926 • Erie, Erie County, Pennsylvania, USA

Age 26 — **Residence**
1930 • Erie, Erie, Pennsylvania, USA
Marital Status: Single; Relation to Head: Daughter

Age 33 — **Departure**
11 Sep 1937 • Hamilton, Bermuda

Age 33 — **Arrival**
13 Sep 1937 • New York, New York

Age 45 — **Residence**
May 11, 1949 • Newfane, Windham, Vermont, USA
Hobby Hill camp advertisement in the Times Record, Troy, N.Y. on May 11, 1949

Age 47 — **Residence**
1951-1953 • New York

Age 52 — **Departure**
5 Jun 1956 • New York, New York, USA
Trip to Denmark with Valborg Rasmussen

Age 63 — **Death of Mother Marie Flint** (1882–1967)
11 Jun 1967 • Erie, Erie, Pennsylvania, USA

Age 81 — **Death of Brother Amos Flint** (1906–1985)
9 Feb 1985 • Erie, Erie, Pennsylvania, USA

Age 90 — **Death of Brother Howard H. Flint** (1910–1994)
28 Jun 1994 • Phoenix, Maricopa, Arizona, USA

Age 90 — **Death**
23 DEC 1994 • New York, USA

Burial
Erie, Erie County, Pennsylvania, United States of America

Appendix 2: Timeline

1931 – YWCA Health Education Director, Schenectady, NY – living at the YWCA

1935 – July 1st Hobby Hill Camp opens in Newfane, VT, ran till September 1st each year

1938 – Ballroom Dance Instructor at Hotel Van Curler, Schenectady, NY – living at 14 Mohawk Ave., Scotia, NY

1941 – fiancé telegram Major James Wilson missing in action

1952 – December 15th purchased 421 Reynolds St., Scotia house from John L. & Lizzie Ulrich

1955 – Hobby Hill Camp closes after 20 years

1956 – June 14th traveled to Denmark by boat with Karen Valborg Sophie Rasmussen, returning by air Sept. 14th

1957 – Opened "Gifts from the Heart" in Scotia, NY – mail order with 10,000 customers in 50 states

25 August, 1959 – 26 August 1962 Beulah H. Hagadorn at 421 S. Reynolds St., Scotia, NY with Billie

1960 – Billie sells Hobby Hill to the Chaffees

1964 – Dancing Teacher bows out after multiple year career

1967 – Starts photography years with many awards & shows

1985 moved to Kingsway Arms Nursing Home

1994 – Billie passes away, Schenectady, New York

Appendix 3: References

1941 Dec 16 AM 1 46 Western Union telegram

April 29, 1942 CHILDREN's EDITION Tinies, Three to Five, Profit from Dance Teacher Says – publication not given

December 16, 1946 The SCHENECTADY UNION-STAR, 'Young Set Guest At Holiday Dance'

January 17, 1949 Cerebral Palsy School Pleasant Valley School, Forest Road, Schenectady, New York letter of thanks

March 26, 1949, SCHENECTADY GAZETTE, 'Miss Flint's Thursday Afternoon Dancing Class Concludes Season With a Party

May 11, 1949 THE TIMES RECORD, Troy, N.Y. Hobby Hill ad for Junior Counselor Training Course – Miss Lillian J. Flint at 14 Mohawk Ave., Scotia 2, New York

1950 'Work and Fun Are One For Miss Flint by Cynthia Dreher Baker (Eleventh in Series) publication not given

Sept 17, 1950 The Erie, PA., SUNDAY TIMES, SUNDAY – 'Silhouette of Success' by Anne Allen

December 28, 1950 SCHENECTADY UNION WOMAN 'Senior Cotillion Held'

March 29, 1952 'Miss Flint's Thursday afternoon dancing class' final dance at the Hotel Van Curler, publication not given

April 15, 1952 'Child's Dance Thursday to Aid CP Fund – publication not given

October 11, 1962 SCHENECTADY UNION-STAR 'Miss Flint's Varied Interests'

1963 Zonta Club Silhouette of Lillian J. Flint by Beulah Hagadorn

September 29, 1964 SCHENECTADY GAZETTE 'Miss Flint Ends 33-Yr. Career – Dancing Teacher Bows Out

December 6, 1975 SCHENECTADY GAZETTE 'Billie Flint's First Photo Show Accents Elves'

May 8, 1976 GAZETTE 'Lillian Flint Photography on Exhibition

November 7 – December 3, 1976 THE FIRST UNITARIAN SOCIETY of Schenectady presents Painting by Mildred Beaudette and A Photographic Exhibit by Lillian Joan Flint 1221 Wendell Avenue, Schenectady, New York

Billy's Christmas 1978 Highlights and Lowlights postcard

November 1979 – Ye Olde Flint Glass-Works - prize winner

December 29, 1979 GAZETTE Picture of the Month 'Japanese Brushwork' by Lillian Flint

1980 Rites of focus on exhibition brochure – Clifton Park at Christ Community Church Reformed "Lillian J. Flint exhibit showing the metamorphosis of the caterpillar to the butterfly photographs

September 18, 1984 GAZETTE - Tales of Old Dorp by Larry Hart – courtesy of the Schenectady Historical Society

December 24, 1994 THE DAILY GAZETTE OBITUARIES 'Billie" Flint 86, was dance instructor and photographer

Made in the USA
Las Vegas, NV
29 May 2022

49503772R10050